Take up
Tennis

Take up Sport

Titles in this series currently available or shortly to be published:

Take up Tennis

Principal contributor:
Anne Pankhurst
LTA Registered Professional and Panel Coach

SPRINGFIELD BOOKS LIMITED

Copyright © Springfield Books Limited and White Line Press
1989

ISBN 0 947655 69 7

First published 1989 by
Springfield Books Limited
Springfield House, Norman Road, Denby Dale, Huddersfield
HD8 8TH

Edited, designed and produced by
White Line Press
60 Bradford Road, Stanningley, Leeds LS28 6EF

Editors: Noel Whittall and Philip Gardner
Design: Krystyna Hewitt
Diagrams: Chris Oxlade

Printed and bound in Great Britain

Photographic credits
Cover photograph: Allsport UK Limited
Supersport Photographs: 6, 10
All other photographs by Noel Whittall

Acknowledgements
Our thanks to the tennis players featured in the photographs:
Liz, Rachel and Oliver Wilson, and Paul Layfield. Liz is an LTA
Professional Coach, and Paul an LTA Intermediate Coach.
Rachel is a Yorkshire County Junior player. Oliver is right at
the beginning of his career...

Contents

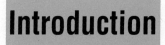

Introduction

Welcome to tennis! You have chosen a game which you can play at almost any age, indoors or outdoors, and anywhere in the world where there is a tennis court. The rules and equipment are the same world-wide, and there are courts in most countries. You can play with just one other person in a game of singles, or with three others in a doubles match. Tennis can be played at the highest competitive level, but is also the perfect game for recreational fun and fitness.

Anyone who can handle a tennis racket can enjoy playing from the very first day. This book will help you learn the basic skills so that you can become a competent player quite quickly. At first, you will simply enjoy hitting the ball back over the net; as your game improves you will want to start learning tactics, refining your shots and playing more competitively.

The more you put into tennis, the better you will become. Once you have developed a taste for playing, you will probably want to join a local club, and soon you will turn into a tennis player, rather than somebody who simply plays at tennis ...

Tennis is not a difficult game to play, but, like any sport, it takes a lot of practice and knowledge to get to the top. This book will help you, but there is no substitute for being taught by a qualified coach; in Britain this means someone holding a Lawn Tennis Association (LTA) qualification. Individual coaching is expensive, but many group courses are held at leisure centres and clubs throughout the country. You can obtain further details from your local authority or the LTA: their address is on page 55.

1

Equipment and clothing

You will learn more easily if you have reasonable equipment. This need not mean spending a lot of money — for example, good-quality aluminium-framed rackets are reasonably priced, yet are perfect for beginners.

Choosing your racket

There is a bewildering array of tennis rackets on the market: they come in a variety of shapes and sizes. Wood is no longer popular: modern frames can be made from aluminium or a number of man-made materials, and strings can be either natural or synthetic — for a beginner, the synthetic variety is better. It will help if you can be guided by a coach or more experienced player when you choose your first racket. While you are learning you do not need an expensive graphite and glass-fibre model, which can cost four or five times as much as an aluminium one.

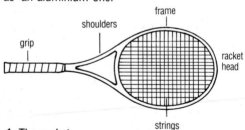

Figure 1 The racket

The most important point is to make sure that the racket's *weight* and *grip* are right for you. Nowadays most full-size models are about the same weight, but the balance can differ considerably. Don't be shy in the shop — try a few practice swings to get the feel of some different rackets. Pay particular attention to the size of the grip. This is where you really can use a *rule of thumb;* when you hold the racket comfortably, your thumb should overlap the nail of your index finger.

This grip is the right size; see how the thumb overlaps the top of the forefinger.

The grip size is usually marked on the handle. The normal range is from one to five: the bigger the number, the larger the circumference of the handle.

Metal or plastic rackets are easy to care for and should give several years of service provided you follow these simple rules:

- Always wipe a wet racket and let it dry before putting it into its case.

- Never leave a racket on the seat or shelf in a car — they do not like heat or strong sunlight.

If one of the strings breaks, or your racket feels "dead" after a season or so of use, it can be re-strung. Go to a qualified stringer, who will be able to advise you on the type of string and tension which will suit your style of play.

Balls

Even for informal practice, buy the best quality balls you can afford. You will need a minimum of four — six is better if you can afford them. You may be able to buy either good quality practice balls or used tournament ones — this is where a friendly coach may be able to help. Always discard balls before they are bald, as they become more difficult to control, particularly in warm weather.

Regulation tennis balls must have a diameter of between $2\frac{1}{2}$ and $2\frac{5}{8}$ in (6.35 and 6.67 cm), and must conform to ITF rules concerning weight and bounce.

Clothing

Gone are the days when you had to wear white to play tennis, although some clubs do still prefer it. Choose light colours for shirts, shorts and skirts. The vital thing is to make sure that your clothes do not restrict your movement in any way. A tracksuit, although not vital, is useful for keeping you warm before and after a match.

Shoes

Good shoes are as important as a good racket, so take extra care when buying them. Tennis shoes are made specially to provide comfort and support as you move forwards, backwards and sideways on the court. They are light and will reduce the risk of injury. Choose a reputable make of shoe and don't "make do" with your old trainers.

Comfortable clothes, with the advertiser's logo prominent, have become a feature of tournament tennis, as Steffi Graf demonstrates.

2

The court

Tennis courts have a variety of playing surfaces, each of which has a different effect on the ball. Tarmac and clay courts tend to give a high bounce and slow the ball down; grass courts give a lower bounce which also varies depending on whether the grass is wet or dry. You may meet a number of different surfaces indoors too, and will soon notice their characteristics. You do not need to worry about these differences at first, but they are worth bearing in mind as your game improves.

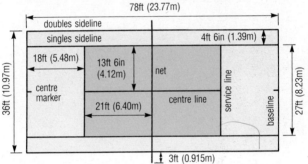

Figure 2 The tennis court

Regardless of the surface, the court should always be the same size as that shown in Figure 2.

The extra lines each side (the "doubles sidelines") are used only for doubles play, and are usually referred to as the "tramlines". The shaded area in the centre indicates the service courts, and is divided by the net.

The net has to be 3 ft (0.915 m) high at the centre, and the posts each side must support the top of the cord 3 ft 6 in (1.07 m) above the ground. It is usual for the same net to be used for both doubles and singles play; however, for singles, additional 3 ft 6 in (1.07 m) supports ("singles sticks") should be placed between the main posts and the singles sidelines.

Full details of the specifications for the court and the net are given in the *Rules of Tennis*.

3

The basic principles and scoring

In this section we see how to play a game of tennis: the rules are explained in their simplest form. For details of the finer points, see chapter 9.

The aim of the game

In the simplest terms, the aim of tennis is to hit the ball over a net into your opponent's territory in a way which makes it impossible for them to hit it back into yours. Each time you do this, you win a *point*; if you win enough points you will soon win a *game*; enough games and you win a *set*, and enough sets and you win the *match*. If you ever find yourself becoming bogged down in the finer points of the game, it is worth remembering that if you can consistently hit the ball once more over the net and into the court than your opponent, you will always win!

Serves and rallies

The ball is put into play when one of the players — the *server* — hits the ball over the net and into the correct service court on the other side. The opponent — called the *receiver* — must let the ball bounce once and then attempt to hit it back over the net. This is called a *service return*, and marks the start of a *rally*. Any series of hits between the players is referred to as a rally.

Once the service return has been made, the ball can be hit before it bounces (a *volley*), or after it has bounced once (a *groundstroke*). Play continues until one of the players hits the ball either into the net or outside the boundary lines of the court, or fails to hit it at all!

Throughout the game, if the ball bounces more than once on your side of the net, you have lost the point.

Rachel opens the service from the right-hand side of the centre mark on the baseline.   ➡

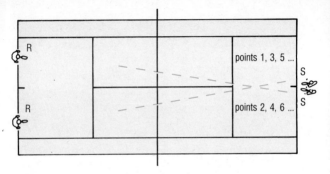

Figure 3 The first service of a match is delivered from behind the right-hand side of the server's baseline. The ball must travel diagonally, and bounce inside the receiver's right-hand service court. The server (S) is allowed two attempts to get the ball "in"; if neither is successful, the receiver (R) wins the point. One player serves throughout each game, and the serves are made from alternate sides of the court. At the end of a game, the right to serve passes to the other player.

Scoring

Tennis has a scoring system all of its own, which you may find odd at first! However, it's quite straightforward and you will not find it hard to learn in practice. The scoring is broken down into manageable portions: points make up games, games make up sets, and sets make up matches. The important thing to remember is that you need to be *two points clear* to win a game, *two games clear* to win a set, and *one set clear* to win a match.

The points a player wins in the game have special names: the players start with no points, which is termed *love*. The first point scored is called *fifteen*, the second is *thirty*, and the third is *forty*, after which may come *advantage* and then *game*. The score of the server is always given first.

Confused? Don't worry — let's see how it works out on the court: in this imaginary example Blue is serving and wins the game:

Blue (server)	Red (receiver)	Score
loses	wins	love–15
wins	loses	15 all
wins	loses	30–15
loses	wins	30 all
wins	loses	40–30
wins	loses	game to Blue

That was straightforward. Now let's watch a game where the score reaches 40 all, and things get a little more complicated:

If the score reaches 40 all, it is called "deuce". The player who wins the next point is said to have the "advantage". If he or she wins the next point as well, the game is won. If not, the score goes back to deuce, and the procedure starts again (this can go on for quite some time). This is how it might have worked out if Red had won the last point in the example above:

Blue (server)	Red (receiver)	Score
loses	wins	deuce
wins	loses	advantage Blue
loses	wins	deuce
loses	wins	advantage Red
loses	wins	game to Red

Ends
The players change ends after the first game of the match and then after every two games for the rest of the match. This ensures that neither player gains an advantage because of the wind or sun or the condition of the court.

The first player to win six games wins a set, provided that the player is two games clear. So if the score reaches 6–5, the set can continue until the score is 7–5 or 8–6, etc. However, to prevent closely-balanced matches from going on for a very long time, the tie-break system can be used (see page 51).

The length of matches
Usually, in both men's and women's tennis, a match is decided over the best of three sets. However, at major championships and internationals the men play the best of five sets.

Doubles differences

So far we have looked at how a tennis match is played between two people – *singles*. When there are four on court – *doubles* – it is a little more complicated.

The doubles court
In doubles play, the full area of the court is used, extending to the outside of the "tramlines". Note that the service courts remain the same size as for singles; the tramline strips only come into play when the service return is made.

Doubles service
The order of service for doubles is more complicated:

● One player serves for each game, and the sides serve alternate games. The order in which the players serve is decided at the beginning of each set and must stay the same until the end of the set. It can be changed in the next set if the players wish.

● Imagine there are two teams, Red and Blue: Red have won the toss and decide to serve first. The service order during the first set would go like this:

First game	Red one
Second game	Blue one
Third game	Red two
Fourth game	Blue two
	and so on...

● Each player on the receiving side receives every *other* service.

● Therefore, you always receive service on the same side of the court throughout a set: so, if you receive the service in the right-hand court at the start, you must continue to do so until the next set at least.

● Once the service has been received, doubles players are free to move anywhere in the court on their side of the net, and may even change sides with each other.

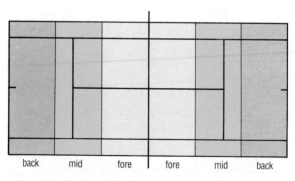

back   mid   fore   fore   mid   back

Figure 4 To help describe the shots, the court is divided into three approximately equal parts: the backcourt, midcourt and forecourt.

4

Playing the game

Having got to grips with the fundamentals of rules and scoring, let's go on court and enjoy learning how to hit the ball. This section will teach you enough to play a reasonable game, and will make a firm foundation for the more advanced techniques.

Don't worry about style too much at first. Simply develop the habit of watching the ball and getting used to the way it bounces. You will soon discover that it is easier to hit if it is a comfortable distance to the side of your body, and will begin to see how important positioning is throughout the game of tennis.

The basic strokes

First, we will explain a few of the terms you will meet as the strokes and techniques are described:

Backhand: When the ball is hit on the opposite side of the player's body to the hand holding the racket.

Forehand: When the ball is hit on the same side of the body as the racket hand.

Grip: When talking about strokes, the *grip* refers to the way your fingers are wrapped around the handle of the racket.

Groundstroke: When the ball is hit after it has bounced once.

Serve: The service stroke, in which the ball is thrown into the air and hit by the server.

Volley: When the ball is hit during a rally before it has bounced.

When describing how shots are positioned, we divide each end of the court into three areas — *backcourt*, *midcourt* and *forecourt*. A ball that *goes deep* is one that travels to your opponent's backcourt.

There are only three basic strokes in tennis — the *groundstroke*, the *serve* and the *volley*. All the other strokes you will meet are variations of these. In the descriptions of the strokes, we give guidelines for when, where and how to play the strokes, but there are no hard and fast rules — playing unexpected shots at unexpected times may win you a lot of points! When you start to play, concentrate on returning the ball; be sure always to watch its flight and bounce very carefully. Your own positioning on the court is much more important at this stage than worrying about style.

The groundstroke

The groundstroke is played on either the forehand or the backhand side of your body. It is a stroke which uses a *swinging* action with the racket, and is easiest to play if you hit the ball when it is a comfortable distance to the side of you, and slightly in front, allowing plenty of room to swing your racket head at the ball. Get the racket moving quite fast and hit the ball with enough power to make it go over the net and a good way into your opponent's court.

As your opponent hits the ball, prepare for your shot by moving into the right position in relation to the ball and getting your racket well back, ready to swing. Be ready to hit the ball at the right time in its flight: if you get too close to the ball, your swing will be cramped; if you get to it too late, your stroke will be uncontrolled. Either way you are unlikely to hit the ball well!

Where and why
As the ball has to have bounced, you usually play a groundstroke in the backcourt or midcourt. You aim to hit the ball deep or wide, making for a difficult return.

When to hit the ball
As a beginner, you will find it much easier to try to hit the ball as it comes down for its second bounce, when it is at a height between your knee and waist. This means that you will have more time to prepare your shot, as the ball will have slowed down after bouncing, and your racket head will be moving up towards the falling ball. As you improve you will find that you are able to get closer to the bounce and hit the ball as it comes up. Hitting this "early" or "rising" ball gives your opponent less time to react.

Remember to try to give yourself enough room to swing the racket, because its head needs to be moving quite fast if you are to hit the ball hard enough to get it deep into your opponent's court. If your arm is tucked into your body, your swing will be cramped.

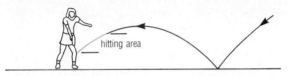

hitting area

first bounce

Figure 5 As a beginner, you will find it easiest to hit the ball as it is beginning to come down — but don't leave it too late!

1 *Paul gets ready to play a classic forehand ground-stroke.*
2 *He starts his swing and watches the ball all the way to the racket.*
3 *Contact is made as the ball is past the top of the bounce.*
4 *The stroke is completed with a fine follow-through.*

1 Paul steps across to play from the backhand.
2 He makes a very full backswing ...
3 ... and hits the ball when it is the perfect distance from his body.
4 The full follow-through is an essential part of the stroke.

Groundstroke grips

The grip for the groundstroke varies slightly between forehand and backhand. We will look at the simple forehand grip first.

When you first pick up a racket, you will almost certainly find that you are using the *eastern* or *shake-hands* grip — it's the natural way to hold it. If you have got it right, the "V" between your thumb and index finger will be pointing straight up the side of the handle.

Some players prefer to hold the racket slightly differently: they use the *semi-western* grip, where the "V" is moved slightly round in the direction of the fingers. Players using this grip find that they have to bend their arm more to hit the ball, and tend to hit it when it has bounced to between waist and shoulder height.

However, the eastern grip is best for you as a beginner, because you can also volley and serve with it, changing only for the backhand.

The eastern grip   *The semi-western grip*

When playing a shot on your backhand side, you use the backhand face of the racket. To allow this, your grip needs to be adjusted so that the "V" is a little further round in the direction of your thumb. The base of the "V" should be in line with the angle of the shaft.

The backhand grip

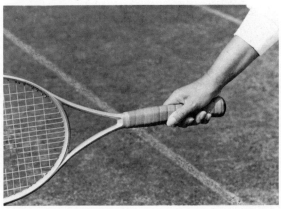

The two-handed backhand grip

You may prefer to use both hands to hit a backhand: if you are going to do this, then you must do it properly! Both your hands *must* be close together on the handle, with your *normal racket hand at the bottom*. This hand can use either a backhand or a forehand grip, while your top hand will usually take up the eastern forehand grip.

The volley

The volley, like the groundstroke, is played either on the forehand or the backhand side of your body, but this time you hit the ball *before* it bounces. The volley uses a *punching*, rather than a swinging, action of the racket.

Aim to hit the ball when it is to the side and slightly in front of you. Take the racket back until it's level with your shoulder and move it firmly forwards to hit the ball, keeping the racket head above the level of your wrist all the time. Your grip and wrist should be firm to stop the racket bucking as you hit the ball.

Don't swing at the ball: you will probably either hit it out of court or miss it completely. Try to concentrate on keeping your racket strings facing your opponent's court — it will stop you from swinging the racket and means that you will hit the ball with a good punching action.

Where and why
Because the ball is hit before it bounces, you will usually play a volley in the forecourt, close to the net. As a beginner, you will be most successful when you can take a ball which is above net-height and hit it downwards into your opponent's court. The volley is an attacking stroke, and you should be trying to win the point outright.

Position makes all the difference when it comes to returning a volley. Here Liz shows what happens if you get too close to the ball: she has to attempt the shot in an impossibly cramped way. Being blinded by the sun hasn't helped, either!

Here Liz is comfortably to the side, so she can reach the ball easily and keep it under control.

When to hit the ball

As a beginner, you will find it easiest to play a volley when the ball is at about shoulder height. Once the ball falls below the height of the net you will have to hit it upwards instead — a much more difficult shot to play, and less effective. Get really close to the net, but be careful — touching the net with your racket or any part of your body is against the rules: if you do so you will lose the point.

Use virtually no backswing with a volley ...

... and very little follow-through.

You will need to move into a position so that you can hit the ball when it is at a comfortable distance to the side and slightly in front of you.

Volley grips

The volley should always be a one-handed stroke, and you can use exactly the same forehand and backhand grips as you do for the groundstrokes. Your grip will need to be tighter than when playing groundstrokes, because the ball will be moving faster — squeeze the handle as you hit.

Some players prefer to use a grip halfway between the eastern grip and the backhand grip, called the *continental*, *chopper* or *service* grip. Its advantage is that it can be used for both forehand and backhand volleys, so there is no worry about changing grips between the two strokes.

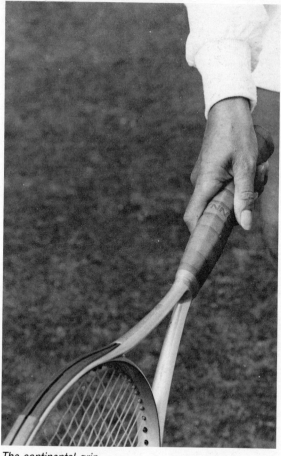

The continental grip

The service

The service is the stroke which is used to start a game. Although the rules allow you to hit the ball with an underarm action, we will describe the more usual *overarm* service:

You toss the ball into the air and hit it with a *throwing* action of the racket before it bounces. There are quite a few rules about the service: at the moment we will only worry about the ones which actually affect how you play the stroke; you can find the rest listed in chapter 9.

The aim of the shot is to hit the ball into the correct service court on your opponent's side of the net, while making it as difficult as possible for it to be returned. The normal way of achieving this is to hit hard and downwards into the service court.

You are allowed two attempts to make your service, called "first service" and "second service". Also, if the ball touches the net on its way into the service court, that serve is called a "let", and has to be taken again.

The service is the one stroke which you make when *you* are ready. It has to be accurate, and you have to be positioned according to the rules. Put *accuracy* before speed and power; it is important to get your services in! If you serve double faults, you not only give that particular point away to your opponent, but also hand over a psychological advantage: double faults are demoralising.

Where to stand for service

When serving, you must stand behind the baseline and either to the right or left of the centre mark. Within these rules, it is up to you to decide where to serve from. In singles, it is usually best to stand close to the centre mark, so that you are in a good position to deal with your opponent's service return. You can stand further out to the side in doubles, because your partner will help you to cover the rest of the court.

The stroke will be easier to play if you stand sideways on to the baseline.

Note that neither of your feet must touch the court in front of the baseline until you have hit the ball.

When to hit the ball

The rules say that you must hit the ball before it bounces. Aim to throw the ball up slowly, so that you hit it at full reach, high in front of you and just towards your racket side. If you are in doubt about whether your throw is correct, check where it lands if you don't hit it: the ball should bounce *inside* the baseline, very slightly to your racket side.

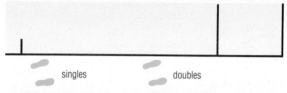

singles   doubles

Figure 6 Usual serving positions for singles and doubles; the foot positions shown are for a right-handed player.

Rachel prepares to serve.

Throwing the ball accurately is vital for a good serve.

How to develop your action

The secret of the overarm service is coordination of the racket movement with the toss of the ball. Your action should start slowly and then explode rapidly as you hit the ball. The trick is to develop an easy rhythm which suits *you*. Often, counting helps as you make the actions of the stroke: *one... two... three....* Alternatively, descriptive words may suit your style better: *down...* as you begin to "place" the ball in the air and start the racket down on its swing; *round...* as the racket is brought round to the "backscratch" position, and *hit...* as you hit the ball just as it starts to fall.

1 *The backswing starts.*
2 *The racket goes into the "backscratch" position.*
3 *She contacts the ball at full speed and full stretch.*
4 *The serve always finishes with a good follow-through.*

As you are aiming to hit the ball *down* into your opponent's court, you should try to hit it from as high as you can comfortably manage.

Once you can be confident of getting your service in, try to hit the ball into the back and to the sides of the service court, where your opponent may not be able to reach it. A serve that is unreturnable in this way is called an *ace.*

Here's what happens if the ball is thrown too far behind your head: Paul has just managed to make contact, but has little control as he loses balance.

Service grip

You can use the normal eastern forehand grip shown on page 21 for your service, but as you get better you should move to the continental or chopper grip.

The ready position

Tennis is a fast-moving game; there is not much time between shots, so you must prepare for the next one as effectively as possible. You do this by returning your racket to a neutral position in front of you whenever possible. This is called the *ready position*.

As you can see, you keep your knees slightly bent, relax your grip, and stay alert! As the racket is in a central position, it is halfway to either a forehand or backhand shot. From the ready position you can respond fast and move to any part of the court for the next ball.

The ready position

While keeping his eye on the ball, Paul uses his hand as a sighting aid when lining up for a smash (see page 41). ➡

Putting it all together

Taking up a good ready position is only a small part of the process of returning the ball successfully. There's a lot more to it than that! The LTA's Coaching Department refers to the package you must develop as the "linked fundamentals", and that sums them up very well. The elements are:

- Watching the ball — all the time: noting both flight and spin.

- Getting your footwork right — the small adjusting footwork which sets you up for your shot, as well as the fast explosive steps which get you around the court.

- Keeping in balance — as you steady-up to hit the ball, and retaining your balance as you make your stroke.

- Controlling the swing and speed of the racket.

- Controlling the racket face as it makes contact.

All these features of your play have to be linked together into a constant smooth performance.

5

Tactics and strategies

However well and consistently you can hit the ball, your shots will be useless without the help of tactics and strategies to help you play a better game. Then you can begin to try to *win* points, instead of just trying not to lose. But always remember that your opponent will be trying the same things against you!

Singles tactics

Keep the ball in play

Remember how the winner is the player who consistently hits the ball over the net one more time than the other? You must use tactics to increase the chances of this being *you*. Obviously it is best to play a shot which is difficult or impossible for your opponent to return. Even if you cannot do this, you should always make an effort to get the ball into your opponent's court somehow. As long as the ball is in play you have a chance of winning the rally; however easy your opponent's next shot seems, a mistake may still be made.

When you are more confident with your strokes and can put the ball where you want in your opponent's court, you can begin to make tactics work for you.

Move your opponent around

Make the game more difficult for your opponent by moving him or her around. This upsets a player's rhythm, and increases the chances of mistakes. Play the ball to various parts of the court, instead of straight to where your opponent is standing:

- Hit towards the sides of the court instead of down the middle
- Sometimes hit to the back of the court, sometimes to the front
- Hit at different strengths, sometimes hard and sometimes less hard
- Hit to "wrong-foot" your opponent

Unfortunately, your opponent will be trying to move you around the court in the same way. *Positioning* is your answer to this...

Keep a good position on court

You should always try to be in a position on the court which allows you to reach as many of your opponent's shots as possible. The obvious place to stand is in the middle, but this does not enable you to reach balls sent behind you, so you have to make a decision: to take up the *attacking* position or the *defending* position.

The *defending* position is about a metre behind the centre of the baseline; from here you have time to react to your opponent's shots.

The *attacking* position is about two metres back from the centre of the net; from here you can volley down into your opponent's court.

Move into one of these positions as soon as you have hit a return: don't wait until your opponent hits the ball — it's too late by then!

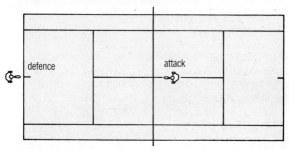

Figure 7 The standard defending and attacking positions

Let's see how it might work when you are out on the court:

During a rally, your opponent plays the ball to your midcourt: this is your chance to come forward into an attacking position. Return the ball into the back of your opponent's court and immediately move forwards to the net. You have played an *approach shot*, and as your opponent's shot comes back, you must be ready to volley the ball out of your opponent's reach. If your volley is weak, the ball will probably be sent past you into your backcourt, leaving you stranded at the net.

It is just as important to be in a good position at the start of a rally. When serving, stand quite close to the centre mark on the baseline, so that you can easily reach a service return which comes down either side of the court.

When receiving service, stand on or just behind the baseline, in the position shown in Figure 8. From here you should be able to reach a service which goes down the centre line or the sideline. For a second service you can move nearer the net — second serves are usually less powerful than first serves.

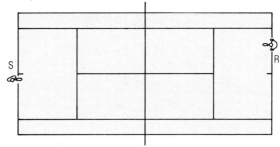

Figure 8 The positions shown here for serving and receiving are usually the most effective.

Play to a weakness

All players have strengths in their games, but most will also have a chink in their armour — the trick is to spot it! For example, if your opponent keeps "running round" his backhand to play a forehand instead, it may mean that his backhand is weak. If you think you have spotted a weakness, play the ball to it, but be careful — give your opponent too much practice and you may find that it becomes a strength instead!

Singles strategies

Different players play the game in different ways: some prefer to serve hard and deep and move to the net to volley straight away; others prefer to play a rally from the baseline, waiting for their opponent to make a mistake and so give them an opportunity to attack. The strategy you use depends largely on your ability and the way you want to play. However, your opponent's style of play, and even the type of court, will have some effect on your overall game plan. There are several factors to try to remember:

● Make sure you win your service game — you should, once you can serve consistently.

● Practise your service return, so that you increase your chance of beating your opponent's serve.

● Some points in the game are extra-important: try to concentrate especially hard on the "big points" such as the first point in a game, which is good to win psychologically, and your first game point.

● *Don't change a winning game.* When your strategies or tactics are working, don't get over-confident and change them. Stay with them until the last point is won. On the other hand, if you are losing, the time has come to try a change, although you should not give up a tactic before it has had time to work.

Doubles tactics

Clearly the tactics which we have described for singles are just as important in doubles, but there are also a few differences to be thought about:

Play as a team
Remember that there are now two of you, and you must support and help each other. If either of you makes a mistake, the last thing that will help is to have a row about it! Try to play with the same partner as often as possible so that you develop an understanding and learn each other's strengths and weaknesses.

Keep a good position on court
Although there are two of you to cover the court, positioning is just as important as it is in singles. Try to get side-by-side on the court as soon as possible, either both in an attacking position at the net, or both behind the baseline. When at the baseline, you should always be trying to create an opportunity to get to the net.

Start each point in the correct position
This is vital. When you are *serving*, stand further to the side of the court than you would in singles, and get to the net as soon as you have served. When your partner is serving, stand at the net in a volleying position on your side of the court.

When you are *receiving*, stand in the same position as you would for singles; when your partner is receiving, stand at the back of the other service court, from where you can move back or forward, depending on the strength of your partner's service return.

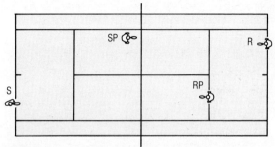

Figure 9 In doubles, correct positioning for service is just as important as in a singles match.
S = server, R = receiver, P = partner

35

For many players this is the heart of tennis: a social match on a summer evening. Note how the server's partner has moved up to the net in the hope of volleying the return.

Play to the weaker opponent

In singles you should play to your opponent's weaknesses; in doubles you should play to the weaker opponent. Make as many of your returns as possible to the weaker player.

Play the angles

Angle your shots across the court to break up your opponents' rhythm and teamwork.

Doubles strategies

As we have seen in singles, it is vital to win your first service game and have the psychological advantage of being in the lead. For this reason, it is usual for the strongest server to serve first. When returning service, keep the ball as low over the net as possible, so that it is difficult for your opponents to volley down at you. Your player with the best return of service should stand in the left-hand court, which is where the service is received for the majority of the game points in a match.

Playing in a team means deciding in advance who will play the balls which go down the middle of the court. Normally, with two right-handed players, it will be the player on the left, who can hit the ball with a forehand stroke. Naturally, the reverse applies if two left-handers are playing. However, if only one of you is left-handed, you will either have two forehands or two backhands in the middle, and which you choose will probably depend on who can best return a wide service on the backhand side.

6

More advanced strokes

Once you have learned the basic strokes from chapter 4, you can begin to develop others which will add some variety to your game.

In this section you will meet the following expressions to describe the way the racket head is angled when you make the strokes:

Open: an open racket is held with the side which will contact the ball facing towards the sky. The angle will vary from stroke to stroke.

Closed: a closed racket faces slightly towards the ground. Again, the angle will vary according to the effect required.

Flat: the face of the racket is square on to the direction the ball is to travel.

Liz shows Oliver the "open" position ...

... and the "closed" position.

Here the rackets are "flat".

The lob

When to use the lob

The lob is used to hit the ball high over the net so that it lands just inside your opponent's baseline. You use it for two main reasons:

- To give yourself time to get back to a good position if your opponent has driven you wide out of court — a *defensive lob*.

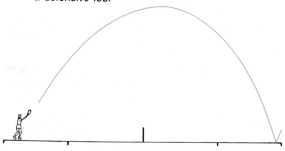

Figure 10 Trajectory of the defensive lob

- To push your opponent back from the net so that you can get there yourself — an *attacking lob*.

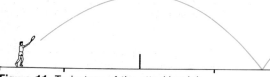

Figure 11 Trajectory of the attacking lob

Where you use the lob

You usually lob from quite close to your own baseline, after the ball has bounced. You can play the lob from the forehand or the backhand.

How to hit the ball

The lob is a form of groundstroke, and you use the same grip and backswing. Remember to keep a comfortable distance between your body and the ball, so that your swing is not cramped. Just before you hit the ball, twist your wrist a little to *open* the face, so that the ball goes up into the air as well as forward. The extent to which you open the face will depend on how high you wish to lift the ball: open it just a little, and you get length as well as height. The more you open the 〔 〕 the higher the ball will go, but its length will

〔 〕 follow-through at the end of the swing,
〔 〕 head will end up higher than for a normal

groundstroke. It is tempting to lean back as you play a lob: try not to, as you can easily lose control of the ball.

Timing the lob
Use the same principle as for the ordinary groundstroke, and hit the ball as it is coming down for its second bounce.

Making the most of the lob
Make sure that you alter the height and position of your lob to suit the effect you need:

● If you are using it *defensively*, you will need to send the ball really high, to give yourself time to get back into position on the court.

● If you are *attacking*, a lower lob is needed, so that it will force your opponent back towards the baseline, but will not allow him or her to get there and wait for the ball!

● Try lobbing to your opponent's backhand — that makes the return more difficult.

The drop shot

As the name suggests, you use the drop shot to "drop" the ball just over the net. It is a useful shot to play against an opponent who likes to stay on the baseline.

Figure 12 Trajectory of the drop shot

Where you use the drop shot
The shot is played from the midcourt, when your opponent is out near the baseline. If you play the shot from the backcourt, or play it too hard, your opponent will have time to "read" the shot and reach the ball.

The grip is the same as for the groundstroke. Begin the swing in the same way too, but bring the racket forward more slowly and try to "catch" the ball on the strings. This will take the speed right off it, and will tend to give it a little backspin (see page 43). The ball should have just enough speed to clear the net and should stop moving forwards when it bounces; if there is enough spin, it might even come back towards the net.

Making the most of the drop shot
The secret of a good drop shot is *disguise*: don't signal your intentions to your opponent; use the normal groundstroke swing and slow down the racket at the last moment. A well-disguised drop shot is almost impossible to return.

The drive volley

The drive volley is a powerful attacking stroke. You hit the ball hard downwards into your opponent's court, before he or she has any chance to reach it. The stroke is a mixture of the swing of the groundstroke and the volley technique of hitting the ball before it bounces. You play it from an attacking position at the net, in answer to to a high, slow ball from your opponent. The drive volley must be hit downwards, so the ball must be above the level of the net when you hit it.

Figure 13 Trajectory of the drive volley

How to hit the ball
Use the same grips that you are using for your normal volley. Take the racket further back than for a normal volley, and *swing* it forward. Keep your wrist firm, and close the face of the racket as it hits the ball.

Timing your drive volley
Because the swing is so important, you need to attack the ball while it is still slightly in front of you, and just to one side.

The stop volley

The stop volley is the volleying version of the drop shot. The idea is to leave your opponent stranded in the backcourt, so the ball should drop just over the net and come to a stop. The ball should be hit when it is level with, or below, the top of the net.

Figure 14 Trajectory of the stop volley

Your position for the stop volley
You should be in the forecourt, close to the net.

How to hit the ball
Use your standard volley grip. Instead of moving the racket forwards to hit the ball, open the face of the racket and move it downwards behind the ball with a short chopping motion. As with the drop shot, this generates *backspin*. The ball should travel upwards and drop just over the net, bouncing quite low. A well-played shot will make the ball bounce back towards the

net slightly. The stop volley, like the drop shot, needs a delicate technique, and will take some practice to master.

Making the most of the stop volley
This is a *gentle* shot. If you play it too deep into the court, there is a great danger that your opponent will be able to return the ball past you.

The smash

The smash is based on the service stroke; it is the answer to a poor lob from your opponent.

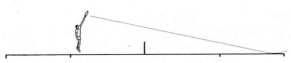

Figure 15 Trajectory of the smash

Where to use the smash
The shot is played in the midcourt before the ball bounces, but you will probably be running back as your opponent will have tried to hit a lob into your backcourt.

Timing your smash
Position yourself so that the ball is falling slightly in front of you and on your racket side. Just as in the serve, you need to hit the ball hard, at as high a point as you comfortably can, so that it goes down into your opponent's court.

The grip for the smash
Use your normal service grip. Now that you have a little experience in the game, you may have found that the continental (chopper) grip suits you better, as it allows you to throw the racket head at the ball more effectively.

Making the most of the smash
Make sure that your arm is at full stretch when you play the stroke, so that you get the maximum advantage from the height. Really *throw* the racket head at the ball, but don't be over-eager. It is very easy to miss your smash! You may find it easier if you sight the ball as it falls towards you, and point at it with your free hand.

7

Introducing spin

As we have seen, *backspin* is a feature of the dropshot and drop volley, which were described in chapter 6, but nearly all the strokes in tennis can be varied by putting spin on the ball. Spin changes both the flight of the ball and its bounce, making it difficult for your opponent to judge the return.

Types of spin

There are three main types of spin: *topspin*, *backspin* and *sidespin*. They each have a different effect on the ball's flight and bounce:

Topspin
A ball with topspin rotates forwards as it travels. The result is that it tends to rise higher off the racket face, but drops sharply at the end of its flight.

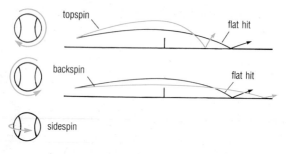

Figure 16 The three types of spin affect the flight of the ball quite dramatically. For the sidespin trajectory, see Figure 17 on page 44.

Note how topspin makes the ball land nearer the net than one hit with similar energy, but without spin (a *flat* hit). The top-spinning ball also "kicks" forwards and upwards when it bounces. Topspin allows you to keep the ball in the court while still hitting it hard.

Topspin is produced by bringing the racket head *up* to the ball and *closing* the face as you strike. For a typical groundstroke, you start with the racket a little lower than usual, and swing it up and over the ball.

Backspin

Here the ball rotates backwards as it travels. The result is that the ball "floats" further than when it is hit with the racket "flat", and slows down when it bounces.

A backspinning ball will tend to travel on quite a low path over the net, but to rise steeply on the bounce. Some slow backspin shots may even bounce back towards the net.

Backspin is produced by hitting the ball with a downward action of the racket head, keeping the racket face *open*. This action is called the *slice*. When you want to use slice on a groundstroke, you start with the racket head higher than the ball, and as you swing the racket forwards, the strings move down the back of the ball. The racket should finish in an *open* position.

Use sliced shots to keep the ball low: this is useful against a volleyer, as low balls are difficult to hit down into your court. It is also a useful way of keeping a baseline player to the back of the court, but take care: it is quite easy to hit your backspin shots out over the baseline.

Sidespin

A ball with sidespin rotates to the left or right as it travels through the air. This makes it swerve in flight and move off at an angle when it bounces. Sidespin is often combined with topspin or backspin.

Sidespin is put on the ball by using a vertical slice action. You will most commonly use it in your serve.

Serving with spin

As your game improves, you will soon realise that if you serve a fault on your first service, it is vital to get the second one in. The temptation is to hit the ball softly to make sure of this, but that will normally be a gift for your opponent. By putting spin on your second service you can both hit the ball harder with confidence, and confuse your opponent. You can also add surprise to your first service by sometimes using spin!

Slice service

As you start your serve, throw the ball up slightly further to your racket side than normal: then throw the racket head forwards and around the outside of the ball as you hit it. The racket should finish past your knee on the other side of your body. The ball should go low over the net and swerve away towards your non-racket side. You may have to alter your aim slightly so that the ball swerves into the service court, and not away out of it!

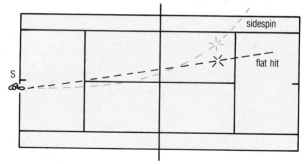

Figure 17 The path of a ball hit with a slice service

Topspin

The topspin serve is a very effective shot. It is more difficult to learn to put topspin on a serve than side-spin, but it is worth the effort. Here's how you do it:

At the start of your serve, place the ball so that it would fall down your back if you failed to hit it. Now bring your racket head up from the "backscratch" position, and throw it *over* the ball. You will discover how to hit the ball so that it clears the net comfortably, then dips down and "kicks" when it bounces. The action is not simple, so don't get disheartened if you find it takes a lot of practice! When you get it right, your opponents will find that they are forced to play the ball at an unexpected and awkward height.

Using spin effectively

Once you have discovered how spin affects the different strokes, you will find that you can use it in many ways:

● topspin on a lob or smash will increase your chances of keeping the ball in court

● backspin often makes those drop shots impossible to return

● sidespin produces a deceptive swerve

● mixing spin with shots which are hit "flat" should confuse any opponent.

8

Fit for tennis

You will enjoy your tennis much more if you keep fit for the game. A match calls for a lot of energy to be used over quite a long period, and you will need:

- *stamina* so that you can keep running through a long game
- *strength* so that you can hit the ball hard
- *suppleness* so that you can reach to hit your shots
- *speed* so that you can move quickly about the court.

Stamina

Regular running, jogging and skipping are excellent ways of building stamina. The accent must always be on *regular* exercise: a huge effort once a week will not be effective, but twenty minutes every day will.

Strength

Although weight-training programmes may be useful for building certain muscle groups in adult players, all strength-training activities should be approached with great care. Children and teenagers should not take part in weight-training programmes while their bodies are still growing, because of the extra danger of damage to the bones and joints. Strength training should always be done under the supervision of an expert: find out more from your coach or club, or your local sports centre.

Suppleness

The following exercises will encourage flexibility and keep you supple: you can use them as part of your warm-up before going on court, or add them to a daily fitness routine. Developing suppleness is the best way of avoiding joint injury during your playing career.

1 Achilles tendon and calf stretch

Stand about a metre from the wall, with the palms of your hands against it. Keeping your feet flat on the ground, slowly bend your elbows until your forearms are flat against the wall. Feel this sorting out your calf muscles! Hold the position for one minute.

2 Twisting tone-up

Sit on the floor with your legs straight. Bend your right knee and put your right foot outside your left knee. Now twist from the waist as far to the right as possible and place your palms on the ground, *keeping your bottom firmly on the floor*. Try to relax your back, and hold the position for a count of ten. Easy. Now change legs and repeat the exercise in the other direction. Now do it all five or ten times...

Speed

You can improve your speed by using sprint training exercises, but remember, you need agility as well as sheer speed. Try some of these exercises regularly:

Tramline shuttle

Run four times across the court as fast as possible, touching the ground between the tramlines with your hand at the end of each run. This is more fun if you can make it into a race with other players.

Foot-length sprints

Make very fast springy steps, but put your foot down so that the heel is level with the other toe. Run across the width of the court like this; it looks absurd, but is a surprisingly strenuous exercise!

High-knee shuttles

Run across the court and back again, using high, bounding strides. Your knees must be raised to waist height at every step.

Number jumps

You need a friend for this. Mark the numbers one to five on the ground in the pattern shown: they should be about two feet (60 cm) apart. Your partner calls the numbers in random order, and you have to jump onto the number as fast as you can. As a variation, the command "left" or "right" is added, and you have to land on the foot specified. Don't make yourself unpopular by chalking the numbers on the court.

Figure 18 Number jumps

Before and after a match

You should always warm up before a match with some gentle jogging and muscle-stretching exercises. This avoids injury to muscles which are unprepared for sudden violent work. Similarly, after the match, put on a tracksuit right away and take some time to cool down. Jogging and stretching is again the best way, so that your body can easily relax into its resting state.

Finally, take a shower and change into fresh clothes as soon as possible.

Players of all ages benefit from a warm-up session before a game.

9

The rules

Here are the main points which you must understand in order to play a game of tennis fairly. They cover most of the situations which may arise during a game, including the tie-break. The full rules, which deal with every possibility and problem, are published by the International Tennis Federation. You can obtain a copy from the LTA, or the governing body of tennis in your country (see addresses on pages 55–56).

"In" or "out"?
The lines that mark the court are treated as part of it, so a ball that touches or overlaps them is in court. Serious competitions have line judges to make the decisions on marginal balls, but in normal friendly play you will have to rely on your own judgement and goodwill.

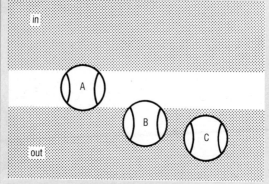

in

out

Figure 19 A and B are "in", but C is "out".

Service rules

● You must serve from behind the right-hand court first, then from behind the left-hand court, and alternate until the end of the game.

- You must stand between the centre mark and the appropriate (singles or doubles) sideline.

- You must not touch the baseline or the ground inside the court until you have served the ball (the service finishes at the moment the ball is hit).

Although Rachel looks as if she might have been over the line, this serve is OK because her forward foot has not touched the court before the ball was hit.

- The ball must not bounce before you hit it.

- Between the start of the service and hitting the ball, you must not change your position by walking or running. You are allowed to make slight movements of your feet, but nothing which really affects your position behind the baseline.

- The ball must land in the diagonally-opposite service court.

- You have two chances to make a successful service, called *first service* and *second service*.

- If the ball touches the net or the cord supporting it, but still bounces in the correct service court, a "let" is called, and the service must be taken again. A "let" does not count as a fault, so that if this happens on your first service, the second attempt still counts as "first service".

- If the ball hits any permanent feature of the court —
such as the net posts — before landing in the
correct service court, the service is a *fault*, not a let.

- If you serve out of turn, or from the wrong court,
the score up to the time the mistake was found still
stands, but the correct order of play must be
resumed immediately.

Rules for receiving service

- The ball must bounce once before you return it; you
are not allowed to volley a service return.

- The server must not serve the ball before you are
ready; however, if it is played too soon, you must
not attempt to hit it, otherwise you will be
considered to have been ready to play.

Rules during a rally

- Always leave a ball which you are sure is going to
bounce out of court: if you attempt a volley return
and fail to get the ball correctly back into your
opponent's court, *you will lose the point*, even
though the shot you hit would certainly have
bounced outside your court. Even if you are
standing outside the lines when you hit the ball,
you still lose the point if you try, but fail, to make
a return.

- If you hit the ball twice in a row deliberately, you
lose the point. An accidental double hit can be
allowed.

- If you touch the net with your racket, or with any
part of your body or clothing, you lose the point.

- If the ball touches the net, cord or posts, while
passing *over* them, provided it falls into the correct
court, it is counted as a good return. Note that the
rule during a rally is different from the rule during
service.

- If you return the ball cleanly around the side of the
net so that it falls inside your opponent's court, the
return is good. However, it must be a clean return:
you are not allowed to bounce it off permanent
fittings such as an umpire's chair!

- If the ball in play hits one lying on the court, play
continues. Only in the rare event of the players or
umpire not being sure which ball was originally in
play is a "let" declared, and the point is played
again.

The tie-break

If it has been agreed in advance, the tie-break can be used to stop matches between evenly-matched players from going on for an unduly long time. It is used to break the deadlock when the score in a set reaches six games all. However, a tie-break is not played in the final set of a five-set match. The scoring follows a simple points system:

Player One, whose turn it was to serve the next game, serves from the right-hand court for one point. Player Two then serves for two points, first from the left court and then from the right. Service then returns to Player One for two points, and so on.

The score is simply the number of points each player has won, the server's score being stated first.

After every six points the players change ends, even though this means that the change will be made between a player's two service points. The service court alternates as usual throughout the tie-break.

The player who reaches seven points first wins the tie-break game, but there must be a margin of two clear points: if there is not, then play continues until either player is two points clear.

The whole tie-break is counted as one game, so the winner's score will be seven games to six, and the players then change ends to start the next set.

10

Tennis for youngsters

There are many opportunities for young people to play tennis these days, and good equipment has been developed to ensure that they are able to enjoy the game from the start.

Short Tennis

For young children, *Short Tennis* is ideal. Although this is played on a small court, using plastic rackets and a sponge ball, all the skills of the full-sized game are introduced. Short Tennis is now being very actively promoted in Britain by the LTA and Slazenger, and many schools and local authorities provide facilities. Children as young as five years old can enjoy the game.

Short Tennis is played on a court the same size as a badminton court. The net is 2 ft 7 in (80 cm) high at the centre, and 2 ft 9 in (84 cm) at the posts. Scoring is by a simple numerical system, the winner being the first to score eleven points. If a match reaches 10–10, play continues until one player has a lead of two points.

Older children

From the age of about eight or nine, children can play tennis on the normal court, but will benefit from using a special junior racket with a short handle.

Star Clubs

The LTA's Junior Star Club programme is a new venture which caters for the needs of young players. There are three grades of club, offering different levels of service, but the object of all of them is to provide tennis-playing youngsters with fun and entertainment at a very reasonable cost. This is the ideal way for children to take up tennis.

3-Star Clubs

These are junior clubs running all the year round under the supervision of a highly experienced coach. They provide coaching for beginners and improvers, regular play, competitions and all the enjoyment of belonging to a club. They are mainly for 8- to 16-year-olds, but Short Tennis for the younger ones (5–9 years) is also available at most of them.

2-Star Clubs

These operate throughout the school summer holidays, and provide coaching for beginners and improvers as well as regular play sessions.

1-Star Clubs

These are short-term clubs which offer a brief introduction to the game and are for beginners only (8 years upwards). Some clubs offer Short Tennis for 5- to 9-year-olds. Courses vary from 6 to 12 hours.

Badge award schemes

Many proficiency badge schemes are operated throughout the world. In Great Britain, the most popular one is the Coca-Cola award scheme, which is promoted through the LTA. The awards are graded from 1 to 6, and are designed to encourage children to keep aiming for the next level of skill in the sport.

For further information about the Junior Star Club Programme and the badge schemes, contact the Lawn Tennis Association at the address on page 55.

Ratings

Ratings are the tennis equivalent of a handicap in golf. You can have a rating regardless of how good or bad a player you are, and will know that when you enter a Ratings Tournament you will play against opponents of equal standard. Ratings originated in France, but the LTA scheme, often referred to as Volkswagen Ratings, after the sponsors, has now been running for some years in Britain. Ratings cover adults and juniors, and the tournaments are proving extremely popular. If you can play tennis at all, do register in the LTA Ratings Scheme and get some tournament experience as soon as you can!

Useful addresses

There are many sources of information about tennis. In the early stages of your game, your local council recreation officer will be able to give you information on public courts and coaching courses. The public library should also be able to help.

As your game improves, you will want to learn more. This is the time to think seriously about joining a club. *Yellow Pages* will list your local ones under "sports clubs". For guaranteed year-round play, contact the nearest indoor tennis centre.

British Isles

The following departments of the Lawn Tennis Association Trust can all be very helpful. Write to them all at:

The Queens Club
West Kensington
London W14 9EG

The LTA Coaching Department: write to this department for lists of coaches in your area; lists of recommended books on playing tennis, practice and fitness training; lists of films and videos about the game; addresses of clubs in your area.

The LTA Tournament and Events Department will supply information on all events, including Ratings Tournaments.

The LTA National Coordinator of Junior Star Clubs has full information on schools tennis, parks tennis and Junior Star Clubs.

Other useful addresses include:

Professional Tennis Coaches Association
21 Glencairn Court
Lansdown Road
Cheltenham
Gloucestershire
GL50 2NB

Irish Lawn Tennis Association
22 Upper Fitzwilliam Street
Dublin 2
Ireland

Scottish Lawn Tennis Association
12 Melville Crescent
Edinburgh
EH3 7LU

Welsh Lawn Tennis Association
National Sports Centre for Wales
Sophia Gardens
Cardiff
CF1 9SW

Overseas

Tennis Australia
Private Bag 6060
Richmond South 3121
Victoria
Australia

New Zealand Lawn Tennis Association
PO Box 11541
Manners Street
Wellington
New Zealand

South African Tennis Union
PO Box 2211
Johannesburg 2000
South Africa

United States Tennis Association Inc
12th Floor
1212 Avenue of the Americas
New York
NY 10036
USA

International

International Tennis Federation
1 Palliser Road
West Kensington
London
W14 9EN